Chocolate Truffles

James Shipley

DEDICATION

This book is dedicated to my Grandmother.
It was through her that I learned the joy of
feeding others. We love and miss you.

CONTENTS

ACKNOWLEDGMENTS

I would like to thank all the people that have made this project possible. In particular, Pam and Joe for believing in me. Lisa for being awesome and helping me format this book. Kathy and Mike Wallace for being supportive of everything I do. My puppy Eowynn (if you have met my dog, you will understand).

Introduction

My fascination with Chocolate started as it has for most, in my youth. When we had an occasion special enough to warrant the purchase of these delectable treats, I was giddy with anticipation. My brothers and I would argue about who got to have what flavors before the box was even opened. The intensity of flavor is one of my most powerful food memories.

It is much the same now. Back then, I didn't understand the different grades of chocolate available and the nuance of taste that comes with a more refined appreciation of chocolate. I still get excited when I try new chocolates. The anticipation, of the first bite and the revelation of what was woven into the ganache, still makes me feel like a young boy waiting for a turn at a piece of candy from the box mother brought home.

My love of chocolate grew even greater after I became a Chef; soon after, I became a Chocolatier as well. After that came chocolate tastings from around the world.

Chocolate is far more than a tasty confection. Its relationship with our lives and food is much more complex than that. The space required to give chocolate its due respect would fill many volumes.

What we shall do here is to take a look at Chocolate as it relates to the fabrication two kinds of truffles, rolled and cast. This guide is meant as an introduction to Chocolates for the beginner and a reference guide for experienced Chocolatiers.

A little history about chocolate.

Chocolate starts with beans of the cacao tree which traces its origins to Central America and played an important role in Aztec and Mayan cultures. They believed that the cacao bean was a gift from the Gods. The beans were used in religious ceremonies and as currency.

When explorers first encountered cacao in Central America, it was nothing like the treat that we are familiar with today. The pods where mashed with water and the drink produced from it was bitter and intense.

It was not until sugar, and later dairy, were added that it became an internationally appreciated food.

Today, cacao is grown in Africa, Asia, and the Americas. There are many varietals of beans that provide nuances of flavor that are sought after by connoisseurs. In the modern world, chocolate is a heavily traded commodity, upon which the livelihood of many relies.

TYPES OF TRUFFLES

In this book we will explore several different kinds of truffles.

The first is a basic rolled truffle. The basic rolled truffle is a medium-consistency ganache that is formed into balls and usually given a powder coating of cocoa powder, ground nuts, coconut, candied zest or other toppings. They are easy to make and deliver a powerful flavor impact.

The second kind is a coated rolled truffle; this is basically the same as the rolled truffle in that it has a medium consistency ganache that is formed into balls. The difference is that before receiving a powder coating, the truffle is dipped into warmed chocolate to give it a firm shell and then rolled in toppings, which also makes the coating adhere to the truffles with greater ease. This method involves a little more work but provides an excellent contrast between firm shell and soft center.

The third kind of truffle is a solid shell truffle, also called a cast truffle. For this method I suggest using polycarbonate molds, particularly a single piece mold. I list reputable vendors in the equipment section of the book.

There are many other aspects of truffle making, decoration and design that demand attention. These will be addressed briefly in a short section at the end of the book, but the focus of this book is to build in you a strong foundation in the basics of chocolate production. We can focus on gilding the lily at a later time.

SELECTING CHOCOLATE

Chocolate vs the other stuff

What counts as chocolate? This question is at the center of a rift between European and American manufacturers. The crux of the argument is cocoa butter. American manufacturers in general have moved to replacing the cocoa butter in chocolate with vegetable oil to increase profits. European producers have strict rules regarding this process.

Much of what Americans consider chocolate may not be called chocolate in Europe. Cocoa butter is essential to great chocolate. When selecting chocolate to work with, you want to look for high cocoa content and no vegetable oil. Much of what many of understand to be chocolate is, in fact, merely chocolate flavored.

While many of us has fond childhood memories of these treats. This book is about appreciating chocolate on a whole other level.

Which one to use? It is important to find a chocolate that tastes great. This is the fun part. Use this as an opportunity to have a great time doing a chocolate tasting party with your friends. You can buy bars of chocolate or little tasting squares from chocolates around the world. Try white chocolates, milk chocolates and dark chocolates from across the globe to find out what you like.

Keep a sheet of paper handy to make notes about the tasting process. I call these tasting sheets. Start with white, then move to milk and finish with dark. As you taste, have everyone write down what they think. There is no right or wrong, it is all about finding out what you really like.

<u>Here are some questions to think about.</u>

How is the color?

The snap of the chocolate?

Are there floral hints in the smell?

What does the smell remind you of?

Let the chocolate melt on your tongue and move it around. How does it feel?

Is it creamy?

Does it linger in the mouth or fade quickly?

What notes do you taste in the chocolate? (does it have notes of fruit or a raisin finish?)

Drink water between each tasting and keep some coffee grounds handy to smell between each tasting to cleanse your palate.

Most importantly, have fun. A chocolate tasting is about experiencing new flavors in chocolate. You can't be wrong, plus you are eating chocolate!

Where do you find a great world selection of chocolates? I have several options for you.

First is to take a look around. There are tons of websites offering great selections from around the world.

Second is to send me an email, and I can put together a tasting box for you. My email address is at the end of the book.

Third is to go to a site I frequently use when I'm itchy for chocolate (I do chocolate tastings every few months to keep my palate sharp).

The website; www.worldwidechocolate.com has loads of sampler packs of chocolates to choose from. You can get individual bars too! I don't get a dime for the shout out. I just love their service.

One final note. When you find the chocolate of your dreams to work with, make sure that it is appropriate for casting if that is your intent. Any chocolate will work for rolled chocolates, but you will want to ask and learn if the chocolate you prefer has the viscosity necessary for tempering and casting. Any purveyor will be able to answer this question for you quite easily. A high cocoa butter content is a very good sign.

DARK CHOCOLATE FORMULAS

Making rolled truffles is easy and fun. The most basic truffle is the rolled truffle; there are endless possibilities with this rustic presentation that allow for your creativity to shine.

Here is a basic dark chocolate formula:

12 ounces bittersweet chocolate (by weight)

Chopped fine, the smaller the pieces the easier the process, go for slivers of chocolate, or use chocolate discos.

3 Tbsp unsalted butter

Unsalted butter give you greater control over the flavor of your truffles, it is worth it.

1/2 cup heavy cream

Get the heaviest cream you can find. 40% or higher is best.

1 Tbsp light corn syrup

Helps to control water content, increasing shelf life.

1/4 cup Grand Marnier or other flavoring

Use strong flavors, marmalades, liquors, etc. Don't go for subtle flavored liquors, they will be overpowered by the chocolate.

1/2 cup Dutch process cocoa powder

Can use ground nuts, coconut, or any other coating you would like. (Try adding spices like cinnamon, cayenne or chili to the cocoa powder)

Step 1:

Place the 12 ounces of chocolate and butter in a medium size glass mixing bowl. Allow to come to room temperature. Microwave on medium heat for 30 seconds and stir well.

Step 2:

Gently heat the heavy cream and corn syrup in a saucepan over medium low heat until it comes to a simmer. If using a flavoring like vanilla bean pods or marmalade, you may add them to the cream while it is coming to temperature.

Step 3:

Remove from the heat and pour the mixture over the chocolate mixture; let stand for 2 minutes. Using a rubber spatula, stir gently, until all chocolate is melted and mixture is smooth and creamy. Gently stir in liquor.

Step 4:

Pour the mixture into an 8 by 8-inch or larger glass baking dish and place in the refrigerator for 1 hour.

Step 5:

Use a melon baller that is the size of the truffles you would like to make and scoop the chocolate onto a sheet pan lined with parchment paper and return to the refrigerator for 30 minutes. Remove the truffles from the refrigerator and shape into balls by rolling between the palms of your hands.

Step 6:

Place the cocoa powder or other coating in a shallow pan. Gently roll each truffle in the coating of your choice and return to pan in refrigerator. Ensure that truffles remain in an airtight container. Chocolate is excellent at

absorbing flavors and will draw in whatever flavors linger if not sealed tight.

Remove from refrigerator 10 minutes before serving to bring close to room temperature. Sealed these truffles will keep for several weeks in the refrigerator and several months if properly frozen. They are best if served within the next few days.

Flavor variations for Ganache

Raspberry (seedless), mix 1/4 cup jam into cream when heating and add 1 Tbsp vanilla extract (instead of liquor) into chocolate mix while adding finished cream mix.

Peanut Butter, mix 1/4 cup of cream all natural peanut (only made from peanuts and perhaps a little salt) butter into chocolate mix instead of liquor.

Orange, use Grand Marnier as the liquor of choice for the basic recipe.

Berry, use Chambord as liquor of choice for the basic recipe.

Jalapeño, add one roughly chopped jalepeno (seeds too) to cream mix and allow to come to simmer then strain and proceed as usual. No liquor required.

Mint, use crème de menthe as liquor of choice for basic recipe.

Mocha, use coffee or cappuccino liquor of choice for basic recipe.

Explore! Try using brandies, port wines, and a wide variety of liquors. Do have a favorite jam or marmalade? Try it out! The markets are full of new and exciting flavors to use for flavorings. Remember that intensity is important if you want your flavor to stand up to the chocolate.

Coated truffles

Here is another option for rolled truffles. Take the chocolate through step 5 then proceed as follows:

The best option is to temper 8 ounces of chocolate as described in the chapter on tempering. For dark chocolate only (not an option for milk and white chocolates), there is another option, it is as follows:

Take 8 ounces (by weight) dark bittersweet chocolate, chopped fine and place into a medium mixing bowl which is sitting on top of another pan with about an inch of water over low heat on the stovetop. The bowl containing the chocolate should not touch the water below. This configuration is called a bain marie.

You may need to adjust the heat up or down. Stirring the chocolate frequently, test the temperature of the chocolate and continue heating until it reaches 90 to 92 degrees F; do not allow the chocolate to go above 94 degrees F. If you do, the coating will not have a nice snap to it when you bite into the chocolate. Once you have reached the optimal temperature, adjust the heat to maintain it.

There are several other options available. The microwave can be used to heat your chocolate. If you choose this route, make sure to use low heat and short bursts of 5 to 10 seconds between stirring and checking temperature. It is more difficult to maintain your temperature once achieved using this method and a small error will lead to a gooey coating that will not give a firm snap.

Another option is to use a heating pan or tempering machine with temperature control built in. These are excellent tools and if you plan on making coated or cast chocolates on a regular basis I strongly recommend getting one. I will list my advice for machine selection in a later selection.

Take your truffles from step 5 and dip them with a dipping fork or use two regular forks to dip your truffle and coat completely. Then place your coated truffles in whatever coating you would like (step 6), or leave them with a crisp dark chocolate outer shell.

MILK CHOCOLATE FORMULAS

Milk chocolates are just as easy to make as dark chocolates. The ratio varies due to the increased amount of dairy and sugar that you find in milk chocolates.

Here is a basic milk chocolate formula:

18 ounces milk chocolate (by weight)

Chopped fine, the smaller the pieces the easier the process, go for slivers of chocolate, or use chocolate discos.

2 Tbsp unsalted butter

Unsalted butter give you greater control over the flavor of your truffles, it is worth it.

1/2 cup heavy cream

Get the heaviest cream you can find. 40% or higher is best.

1 Tbsp light corn syrup

Helps to control water content, increasing shelf life.

1/4 cup Grand Marnier or other flavoring

Use strong flavors, marmalades, liquors, etc. Don't go for subtle flavored liquors, they will be overpowered by the chocolate.

1/2 cup Dutch process cocoa powder

Can use ground nuts, coconut, or any other coating you would like.

Step 1:

Place the 18 ounces of chocolate and butter in a medium size glass mixing bowl. Allow to come to room temperature. Microwave on medium heat for 30 seconds and stir well.

Step 2:

Gently heat the heavy cream and corn syrup in a saucepan over medium low heat until it comes to a simmer. If using a flavoring like vanilla bean pods or marmalade, you may add them to the cream while it is coming to temperature.

Step 3:

Remove from the heat and pour the mixture over the chocolate mixture; let stand for 2 minutes. Using a rubber spatula, stir gently, until all chocolate is melted and mixture is smooth and creamy. Gently stir in liquor.

Step 4:

Pour the mixture into an 8 by 8-inch or larger glass baking dish and place in the refrigerator for 1 hour.

Step 5:

Use a melon baller that is the size of the truffles you would like to make and scoop the chocolate onto a sheet pan lined with parchment paper and return to the refrigerator for 30 minutes. Remove the truffles from the refrigerator and shape into balls by rolling between the palms of your hands.

Step 6:

Place the cocoa powder or other coating in a shallow pan. Gently roll each truffle in the coating of your choice and return to pan in refrigerator. Ensure that truffles remain in an airtight container. Chocolate is excellent at

absorbing flavors and will draw in whatever
flavors linger if not sealed tight.

Remove from refrigerator 10 minutes before
serving to bring close to room temperature.
Sealed these truffles will keep for several
weeks in the refrigerator and several months if
properly frozen. They are best if served
within the next few days.

Flavor variations for Ganache

Raspberry (seedless), mix 1/4 cup jam into cream when heating and add 1 Tbsp vanilla extract (instead of liquor) into chocolate mix while adding finished cream mix.

Peanut Butter, mix 1/4 cup of cream all natural peanut butter into chocolate mix instead of liquor.

Orange, use Grand Marnier as the liquor of choice for the basic recipe.

Berry, use Chambord as liquor of choice for the basic recipe.

Jalapeño, add one roughly chopped jalepeno (seeds too) to cream mix and allow to come to simmer then strain and proceed as usual. No liquor required.

Mint, use crème de menthe as liquor of choice for basic recipe.

Mocha, use coffee or cappuccino liquor of choice for basic recipe.

Explore! Try using brandies, port wines, and a wide variety of liquors. Do have a favorite jam or marmalade? Try it out! The markets are full of new and exciting flavors to use for flavorings. Intensity is still important if you want your flavor to stand up to the chocolate, but milk chocolate will allow for more versatility in flavors, try Kahlua, Frangelico or Irish Cream.

Coated truffles

To coat your truffles. Temper 12 ounces of milk chocolate according to the directions in chapter on tempering milk chocolate. When your coating chocolate is in temper:

Take your truffles from step 5 and dip them with a dipping fork or use two regular forks to dip your truffle and coat completely. Then place your coated truffles in whatever coating you would like (step 6), or leave them with a crisp milk chocolate outer shell.

WHITE CHOCOLATE FORMULAS

White chocolates are easy to make and offer a wider variety of flavors. You can use much more subtle flavors when working with white chocolate. For example, light citrus flavors, mild liquors like Limoncello, or apricot jam.

Here is a basic white chocolate formula:

24 ounces white chocolate (by weight)

Chopped fine, the smaller the pieces the easier the process, go for slivers of chocolate, or use chocolate discos.

2 Tbsp unsalted butter

Unsalted butter give you greater control over the flavor of your truffles, it is worth it.

1/2 cup heavy cream

Get the heaviest cream you can find. 40%
or higher is best.

1/4 cup Grand Marnier or other flavoring

You can use a wide variety of flavorings
with white chocolate. Subtle flavors work
too. White chocolate will lend its palate
to your flavor.

1/2 cup Dutch process cocoa powder

Can use ground nuts, coconut, or any
other coating you would like.

Step 1:

Place the 24 ounces of chocolate and butter in a medium size glass mixing bowl. Allow to come to room temperature. Microwave on medium heat for 30 seconds and stir well.

Step 2:

Gently heat the heavy cream and in a saucepan over medium low heat until it comes to a simmer. If using a flavoring like vanilla bean pods or marmalade, you may add them to the cream while it is coming to temperature.

Step 3:

Remove from the heat and pour the mixture over the chocolate mixture; let stand for 2 minutes. Using a rubber spatula, stir gently, until all chocolate is melted and mixture is smooth and creamy. Gently stir in liquor.

Step 4:

Pour the mixture into an 8 by 8-inch or larger glass baking dish and place in the refrigerator for 1 hour.

Step 5:

Use a melon baller that is the size of the truffles you would like to make and scoop the chocolate onto a sheet pan lined with parchment paper and return to the refrigerator for 30 minutes. Remove the truffles from the refrigerator and shape into balls by rolling between the palms of your hands.

Step 6:

Place the cocoa powder or other coating in a shallow pan. Gently roll each truffle in the coating of your choice and return to pan in refrigerator. Ensure that truffles remain in an airtight container. Chocolate is excellent at

absorbing flavors and will draw in whatever flavors linger if not sealed tight.

Remove from refrigerator 10 minutes before serving to bring close to room temperature. Sealed these truffles will keep for several weeks in the refrigerator and several months if properly frozen. They are best if served within the next few days.

Flavor variations for Ganache

Raspberry (seedless), mix 1/4 cup jam into cream when heating and add 1 Tbsp vanilla extract (instead of liquor) into chocolate mix while adding finished cream mix.

Blueberry, mix 1/4 cup jam into cream when heating and add 1 Tbsp vanilla extract (instead of liquor) into chocolate mix while adding finished cream mix.

Orange, use Grand Marnier as the liquor of choice for the basic recipe.

Berry, use Chambord as liquor of choice for the basic recipe.

Lemon, add zest of 2 lemons to cream as it simmers and then strain. Instead of liquor add 2 Tbsp lemon extract to mix.

Mint, use crème de menthe as liquor of choice for basic recipe.

Coconut, use 1/4 cup coconut liquor and finish with rolling in toasted coconut flakes.

Explore! Try using brandies, port wines, and a wide variety of liquors. Do have a favorite jam or marmalade? Try it out! The markets are full of new and exciting flavors to use for flavorings. White chocolate does not have the strong flavor that dark and milk chocolates convey and is therefore receptive to more subtle flavorings, try citrus elements and consider candied minced zest for a finishing coat.

Coated truffles

To coat your truffles. Temper 16 ounces of white chocolate according to the directions in chapter on tempering white chocolate. When your coating chocolate is in temper:

Take your truffles from step 5 and dip them with a dipping fork or use two regular forks to dip your truffle and coat completely. Then place your coated truffles in whatever coating you would like (step 6), or leave them with a crisp white chocolate outer shell.

TEMPERING CHOCOLATE

Seed Method:

There are several ways to temper chocolate. In this book we will address seed tempering. It is the easiest and most consistent method to use.

This method assumes the use of a bain marie (double boiler) to melt the chocolate. The chocolate should be at room temperature (68 to 70 degrees) before starting.

Step 1:

Make sure that your chocolate is finely chopped or in discos form. Reserve 1/3 of the chocolate you plan to temper. The remainder is melted in a double boiler to no more than:

120°F (for dark chocolate)

115°F (for milk chocolate)

110°F(for milk chocolate)

Above these temperatures the chocolate may separate and become unusable. If your chocolate separates. Don't worry, discard it and try again.

Step 2:

Add the reserved chocolate into the mix and stir to combine. This introduces the stable structure of the tempered chocolate you added to the molten chocolate which is looking for structure. Finely chopped chocolate will mix easier and provide greater distribution of the correct crystalline structure. Keep stirring rapidly and check its temperature frequently until the proper one is reached.

82°F (for dark chocolate)

80°F (for milk chocolate)

78°F (for white chocolate)

Step 3:

Reheat the chocolate to complete the tempering process. The reheating melts any of the undesirable crystals that are formed in cooling. When it reaches the desired temperature

88-90°F (dark chocolate)

86-88°F (milk chocolate)

82-84°F (white chocolate)

the chocolate is now tempered. If the temperature rises above these recommended temperatures, you may need to start the entire process over again. Therefore, pay close attention to maintaining temperature.

Step 4:

Checking temper. Even though you have done everything according to directions it is still necessary to check and make sure the chocolate is back in temper. An easy way of checking if the chocolate is in temper, is to apply a small quantity of the chocolate to a scrap of parchment or wax paper, wait five minutes, and then try to peel the chocolate from the paper. If you can, and it's not blotchy, you are good to go. If not, start the process over. One big variable that affects this process is the temperature of your workplace. Try to keep it in the 68 to 72 degree range.

Step 5:

Maintain the temperatures achieved in Step 3. Exceeding these temperatures may cause your chocolate to come out of temper. If you chocolate cools a few degrees too low you may reheat it multiple times back to the proper "temperate zones" indicated in Step 3.

If the chocolate cools to the point of hardening, the tempering process must start again.

A few final tips for success:

Always use an accurate thermometer, and keep the temperature low; Always work in a cool environment with relative humidity of 50% or lower (our Indoor Humidity Monitor shows room temperature & humidity as well as highs and lows)

Always test for temper, using a piece of parchment or wax paper.

Don't worry and have fun, if the chocolate goes out of temper, you can always start over, you didn't hurt anything.

USING A MACHINE

When I first began experimenting with making chocolates, I didn't even know that I was supposed to use a bain marie. I made them over direct heat. It was very difficult and I made loads of mistakes.

If you plan on mainly making rolled truffles then a tempering machine is definitely not the choice for you. It is simply not necessary.

Using a tempering machine takes much of the humdrum work of cast chocolate truffle design away and lets you focus on the design of ganache and decoration of the final product.

If you are planning on making cast truffles on a regular basis then investing in a machine is a great idea.

Fortunately tempering machines are not expensive, there are lots of great options for under five hundred dollars. I don't recommend merely buying a heating unit because they lack the versatility of tempering machines, which can also be set to keep certain temperatures.

The advantage of a machine is that it monitors heat, time and stirs the chocolate the entire time. Most machines will even tell you when it is time to add the seed chocolate.

It is important to note, however, that machines are not perfect. The temperature of your work area and the humidity in the room can affect the temper of your chocolate. Make sure that you check the final temper of your chocolate. Remember, the machine is not the final arbiter, you are. It is merely another tool, although a very groovy one.

In the section on equipment I share my experience with tempering machines and give my personal recommendation.

CASTING TRUFFLES

This technique presumes the use of a hard truffle casting, preferably a polycarbonate mold, types and sources of which are discussed in the chapter on Equipment leads.

When preparing to cast truffles it is essential to have all your equipment at the ready because the casting must happen quickly for the best results.

You will need to have your chocolate mold ready. An important note regarding chocolate molds. **Do not ever use soap on your molds**, they should be rinsed clean using warm water and if absolutely necessary a very soft wash cloth. After several uses, the cocoa butter from your castings will build in the mold and your chocolates will have a beautiful shine. Using soap strips this cocoa butter and will make your next batch of chocolates taste like soap. Avoid anything abrasive on your molds, because small scratches will a poor appearance in your finished product and will make it harder to release the truffles from the mold. Your mold should be clean and dry before each use.

You will need:

large plastic spoon (very large), or ladle

pastry or bench scraper

piping bag or ziplock bag

parchment or wax paper.

Set out a large work area and place a two foot length piece of parchment or wax paper on your work surface.

When casting you want to work as quickly as possible and don't forget to stir your tempered chocolate frequently during the process if you are hand tempering.

The ideal temperature of your workspace should be approximately 68°F or a close as possible.

Try and make sure that your mold cavities are the same temperature as your chocolate when you fill them. Use a hair dryer (used only for food) to quickly warm the mold cavities or store the molds in a warm place, but not warmer than the chocolate you have tempered. You want the molds approximately the same temperature as your chocolate. Chocolate placed in a cold mold will not set properly, the mold should be at least slightly above room temperature.

Using a large plastic spoon or ladle, fill the mold with tempered chocolate. Then hold the mold by the edges and shake and tap (vibrate) the mold against the work surface to settle the chocolate into the cavities and to reduce the risk of small bubbles marring the mold detail. Let the coating set for about 1 minute.

Turn the filled mold upside down over the parchment or wax paper and move in a vigorous figure eight pattern to remove all but a thin shell of chocolate in the mold cavities (about 1 minute). This is why the process is called "shell" casting.

Turn the mold over and using a pastry or bench scraper, scrape off the excess chocolate from across the top of the mold. This motion should be completed with a single broad stroke across the mold surface. A little of the scraped chocolate might fall back into the cavities but that is ok. Chocolate removed during this stage can be put back into the tempered chocolate you have either in a bain marie or tempering machine.

Allow the molded shell to harden at room temperature. Set the mold opening side up and let set for 5 to 10 minutes.

Filling the molds. When filling cast chocolates, you should not refrigerate the ganache until completely cooled. You want the ganache just fluid enough to pipe, but not warm enough to melt the chocolate mold (no more than 70 degrees).

When the chocolate lined shells have hardened, take the ganache they you have made and place in either a piping bag or ziplock bag and nip the end to make a small hole to pipe the chocolate into the shell. Place the tip at the base of the shell and fill until the mold is 3/4 full. Try not to get any filling on the outer rim of the chocolate.

If you do get filling on the edge of the chocolate shell scrape it off immediately as it will keep your chocolate bottom from adhering properly.

If your centers are very soft, you will need to let them set until the ganache becomes firm enough to support the final layer of chocolate that will form the bottom of your finished truffle.

The final step is the bottoming of the mold. Use your hair dryer (used only for food) to quickly warm the edge of the chocolate coating so it will adhere to the bottoming chocolate. Try two slow passes on low heat from about two feet away. Over time, experimentation will help you to find the ideal technique. The greatest danger is overheating the chocolate shell and ruining the temper, so err on the side of caution if uncertain.

Pour or ladle chocolate across the top of the filled mold and lightly vibrate the mold for about 10 seconds to let the chocolate settle into the shells. Then scrape a pastry or bench scraper across the top at a 90 degree angle you will get a flat top. This should be done in a single stroke.

Let chocolates sit at room temperature for 10 minutes. If after this time the chocolates do not appear to be pulling away from the mold slightly, you may cover the mold with a piece of shrink wrap and set it in the refrigerator for up to 5 minutes.

Once you think that the mold is ready, turn the mold over on parchment or wax paper. If your chocolate is tempered properly and it is completely hardened, the chocolates should just fall out of the mold. If they don't fall out give the mold a little tap on the bottom to help release the chocolates. If they don't fall out, it may be that you have excess chocolate on the bottoms of the shells that is holding them in place. You will need to tap the mold firmly to release the shells if this is the case. If that doesn't work then set them aside and try again in five minutes.

If not serving immediately, place chocolates in an airtight container and store in the refrigerator for up to 3 weeks.

Remove any remaining chocolate from your work surface and reserve for future use. Leftover ganache can be refrigerated or even frozen (if double bagged) and kept for future use.

EQUIPMENT LEADS

In the section on casting chocolates, there is a fair amount of equipment mentioned that may or may not be available locally. Here are my recommendations on sourcing some of that equipment. Keep in mind, these are the recommendations based on my years of working with different vendors. I have not been remunerated in any way for these endorsements.

Pastry or bench scrapers

Dipping forks

Polycarbonate molds

Thermometers (candy or laser)

I recommend using a website called: www.chefrubber.com for purchasing these items. They have a great inventory of fantastic molds. Stay with the single piece polycarbonate molds until you become more comfortable casting chocolate, then consider using the molds compatible with transfer sheets or look into their excellent selection of cocoa butter paints. If you have questions about molds, the staff is very knowledgeable about their products and can guide you to the right kinds of molds for your needs.

There are a wide variety of tempering machines available. While I have used many of those, I am not familiar with every kind. I have worked with one company in particular and have been impressed not only with their products but by their extremely attentive and supportive customer service staff. That company is at www.chocovision.com They have excellent tempering machines that are very low maintenance. I personally purchased a Revolation 2 several years ago and it has performed admirably. When I accidently damaged the machine, the customer service and repair team that worked with me was amazing. They will be my choice for tempering machines for the rest of my chocolate making career.

More Ganache Recipes

As you progress in making rolled and cast truffles, you will begin to experiment with the ratios involved. This is when magic happens. There aren't really any rules when it comes to making a great ganache. Feel free and mix and match. Imagine a lemon white chocolate ganache enrobed in a dark chocolate shell. Yummy.

Some basic formula changes that you may encounter revolve around the addition of corn syrup to ganache recipes. If you are adding a jam, marmalade or other sweetened flavor then omitting the corn syrup is a good idea. Additionally, since not all chocolates are created equal, you may focus on a milk chocolate that has a higher sugar content. You will have to use your judgment to decide if adding corn syrup is reasonable.

If you are looking to add a little something special to your ganache, try replacing 1/4 to 1/2 of the volume with crème fraiche. This will add a nice finish to your chocolates. I particularly enjoy this with dark chocolate.

Okay here are some more ideas for flavoring ganache.

Flavor variations for Ganache

Amaretto use Amaretto as the liquor of choice for the basic recipe.

Tea, steep two bags of your favorite tea in the cream as it comes to temperature. Remove and omit liquor.

Jams, Marmalades and Honey instead of ganache, how about filling as cast truffle with one of these?

Cinnamon, add 1 tsp cinnamon to cream and use a cinnamon liquor of choice for the basic recipe.

Vanilla, add scraped seeds of two vanilla beans to cream as it simmers and then strain. Instead of liquor add 2 Tbsp vanilla extract to mix.

Green Faeries, use Absinthe as liquor of choice for basic recipe.

Ginger, use 1/4 cup finely minced candied ginger and add to cream. Omit liquor. Roll finished truffle in light dusting of candied ginger.

Gianduja, add 1 cup of lightly toasted and finely ground hazelnuts (in a food processor or spice mill) great with dark or milk chocolate. Omit liquor or use a hazelnut liquor for added punch.

Baileys, add 1/2 cup baileys to your milk chocolate ganache.

Maple, add 1/4 to 1/2 cup maple syrup to white chocolate instead of liquor.

Here is a caramel recipe that makes a great filling for cast truffles. It can also be added to ganache for a caramel/chocolate mix.

Chef Shipley's Caramel

2 cups sugar
1 tsp corn syrup
10 oz heavy cream
1 Tbsp vanilla extract
1Tbsp fresh lemon juice
1 pinch salt (kosher)
1 Tbsp butter (unsalted)

Put 2 cups of sugar in a saucepan, add enough water to make sugar look like wet sand. Add 1 tsp corn syrup. Put on medium heat and do not stir. Meanwhile heat the cream in the microwave for 1 minute on high and add all other ingredients to it except the butter. The sugar will bubble down and will begin to brown. When it is a light amber color, remove from heat and add the cream, butter, lemon juice, vanilla extract and salt. Be very careful! It is easy to burn yourself during this phase. Gently whisk to combine. Let cool.

I hope that these examples give you an inkling of the range of options that lies before you. I have omitted much because this book is meant to be an introduction to creating truffles, not a comprehensive guide. You now have enough information to branch out and begin to discover your own flavors. Feel free to email me with questions too! I would love to hear what you have created. Please let me know. Send pics of what you have made!

Here is my email:
twobearschocolates@gmail.com

OTHER BOOKS BY JAMES SHIPLEY

The Artisans Cookbook
The 24 Day Challenge Cookbook
Cute Cat and Kitten Jokes
Inspiration to Run
It's Raining Cat and Dog Quotes
The Bear Mindset for Success